# Touching the Soul...

## Connecting through Poetry

by

Margaret M. Desjardins

CreateSpace Independant Publishing Platform,
North Charleston, SC

Printed in the U.S.A. by CreateSpace,
North Charleston, SC

Touching the Soul...  Connecting through Poetry
ISBN - 13: 978-0692296677 (Egg Rock Publishing)
ISBN - 10: 0692296670
Library of Congress Control Number:
LCCN: 2014916976


Printed in November 2014

EGG ROCK PUBLISHING LLC

# Table of Poems

*Introduction* .......................................... ix

*Part I – Taking Your Breath Away* ............. xi

*Wake up the Dawn* .................................... 1
*Through the Looking Glass, Tableside* ................. 2
*Two Gray Squirrels* .................................... 3
*Summer's Slide* ...................................... 4
*Autumn's Light* ...................................... 5
*Autumn's Gift* ....................................... 6
*Autumn declares itself…* ............................. 7
*Autumn Stomping* .................................... 8
*Shooting Star* ....................................... 9
*Falling Leaves* ...................................... 10
*Raking Leaves…* ..................................... 12
*Sky Screen* ......................................... 14
*A Flower Grows* ..................................... 15
*Cracking Dawn* ..................................... 16
*Summer Sunset* ..................................... 17
*Eating Ice Cream* ................................... 18
*FOG…* .............................................. 19
*Stillness in the Georgian Valley* ..................... 20
*Liquid Sunshine…* ................................... 21

*I Will Go Walking* . . . . . . . . . . . . . . . . . . . . . . . . . . . . . . . . . . 22

*Enticing my senses* . . . . . . . . . . . . . . . . . . . . . . . . . . . . . . . . . 24

*A Subtle Withdrawal* . . . . . . . . . . . . . . . . . . . . . . . . . . . . . . . . 25

*Night Falls* . . . . . . . . . . . . . . . . . . . . . . . . . . . . . . . . . . . . . . . . 26

*Veiled beauty* . . . . . . . . . . . . . . . . . . . . . . . . . . . . . . . . . . . . . . 27

*Part II – In Love* . . . . . . . . . . . . . . . . . . . . . . . . . . . . . . . . . 29

*Wallowing in Could and Should* . . . . . . . . . . . . . . . . . . . . . . 31

*Ping-Ping!!* . . . . . . . . . . . . . . . . . . . . . . . . . . . . . . . . . . . . . . . 32

*Barricade Stormer* . . . . . . . . . . . . . . . . . . . . . . . . . . . . . . . . . 34

*Complicated* . . . . . . . . . . . . . . . . . . . . . . . . . . . . . . . . . . . . . . 35

*Searching...* . . . . . . . . . . . . . . . . . . . . . . . . . . . . . . . . . . . . . . . 36

*Valentine's Day* . . . . . . . . . . . . . . . . . . . . . . . . . . . . . . . . . . . . 39

*Nameless at the Landings Bar* . . . . . . . . . . . . . . . . . . . . . . . 40

*A Prisoner Affixed* . . . . . . . . . . . . . . . . . . . . . . . . . . . . . . . . . 41

*Without Like...* . . . . . . . . . . . . . . . . . . . . . . . . . . . . . . . . . . . . 42

*Pub Talk* . . . . . . . . . . . . . . . . . . . . . . . . . . . . . . . . . . . . . . . . . 44

*Part III – And It Hurts* . . . . . . . . . . . . . . . . . . . . . . . . . 47

*I WEEP* . . . . . . . . . . . . . . . . . . . . . . . . . . . . . . . . . . . . . . . . . . 49

*Lollipops* . . . . . . . . . . . . . . . . . . . . . . . . . . . . . . . . . . . . . . . . . 50

*Womb Raiders* . . . . . . . . . . . . . . . . . . . . . . . . . . . . . . . . . . . . 51

*Forgiveness* . . . . . . . . . . . . . . . . . . . . . . . . . . . . . . . .        . . . . . . . . 52

*Surrender* . . . . . . . . . . . . . . . . . . . . . . . . . . . . . . . . . . . . . . . . 53

*Too Busy to Notice* . . . . . . . . . . . . . . . . . . . . . . . . . . . . . . . . 54

*Relic Fragile Now* . . . . . . . . . . . . . . . . . . . . . . . . . . . . . . . . . 55

*Disconnecting* ..................................... 56

*Forbidden* .......................................... 57

*Beaten* ............................................. 58

*Vulgarity's Abrasive Master* ........................ 59

*Mental Break-down...* ............................... 60

*Divisible* .......................................... 61

*Ravages of War* ..................................... 62

*Cruelty of Time* .................................... 63

*Is Anybody Out There?* .............................. 64

*A Free-Wheeling Life...* ............................ 66

*Part IV – Challenging the Status Quo*........ 69

*"The Stir"* ......................................... 71

*In Sync ...* ........................................ 72

*Boxes of Wishes* .................................... 73

*Unfolding Regret* ................................... 74

Dark *Demons Within* ................................. 75

*Ordinary People Crushed* ............................ 76

*Fading Wish* ........................................ 78

*Undo the Did? Never!* ............................... 79

*Ugly Sheep* ......................................... 80

*Collision of Worlds (Ferro painting)* ............... 82

*Kneading Bread* ..................................... 84

*New England Giant Pumpkin Weigh-In
(at the Topsfield Fair)* ............................. 86

*All That Matters...* ................................ 87

*What's All the Fuss About?* . . . . . . . . . . . . . . . . . . . . . . . . . 88

*Stepping Out* . . . . . . . . . . . . . . . . . . . . . . . . . . . . . . . . . . . 92

*Transformation* . . . . . . . . . . . . . . . . . . . . . . . . . . . . . . . . . 93

*YOLO, YOLO* . . . . . . . . . . . . . . . . . . . . . . . . . . . . . . . . . . . 94

*Dissolving Boundaries* . . . . . . . . . . . . . . . . . . . . . . . . . . . . 95

*Be still, the Lie* . . . . . . . . . . . . . . . . . . . . . . . . . . . . . . . . . . 96

*Blurred Vision* . . . . . . . . . . . . . . . . . . . . . . . . . . . . . . . . . . 97

*Wandering toward Nothingness...* . . . . . . . . . . . . . . . . . . 98

*Struggling for the Right Fit* . . . . . . . . . . . . . . . . . . . . . . . 99

# *Part V - Remembering Place* . . . . . . . . . . . . . . . . 101

*In the Underworld of Dust and Goo* . . . . . . . . . . . . . . . . 103

*Two Perspectives:* . . . . . . . . . . . . . . . . . . . . . . . . . . . . . . . 104

*Sail Away (Light)* . . . . . . . . . . . . . . . . . . . . . . . . . . . . . . . 104

*Sail Away (Dark)* . . . . . . . . . . . . . . . . . . . . . . . . . . . . . . . 105

*Friendship's Gift* . . . . . . . . . . . . . . . . . . . . . . . . . . . . . . . 106

*New England Rock Walls* . . . . . . . . . . . . . . . . . . . . . . . . . 107

*Separating Boundaries* . . . . . . . . . . . . . . . . . . . . . . . . . . 108

*Stone Walls* . . . . . . . . . . . . . . . . . . . . . . . . . . . . . . . . . . . 110

*A New England Sea Town* . . . . . . . . . . . . . . . . . . . . . . . . 111

*Yankee Farmers* . . . . . . . . . . . . . . . . . . . . . . . . . . . . . . . . 112

*A Muted Shade of Motley Memories* . . . . . . . . . . . . . . . . 114

*Island Memories...* . . . . . . . . . . . . . . . . . . . . . . . . . . . . . 115

*Settling In* . . . . . . . . . . . . . . . . . . . . . . . . . . . . . . . . . . . . 116

*A Lighthouse Stands* . . . . . . . . . . . . . . . . . . . . . . . . . . . . 117

*Tucked In—Nantucket* .............................118

*??? It is difficult to think of...???* ...................119

*Moving Boxes...* ...................................120

*Correspondence ON Simply Thanks!!!!!!* .............122

*Bleak Misery* .....................................123

*Ancestral Sweeps...* ...............................124

*Dark Memories* ...................................126

*Dreamy* ..........................................127

*Something Lost Is Something Not Found* ...........128

*Part VI - Waxing Nostalgic* ..................131

*When All Is Still* ..................................133

*Summer's Slide* ...................................134

*Nostalgia Reinvented* .............................135

*The Clarity of Loss* ...............................136

*The Lady in Black* ................................137

*Standing Here...* ...................................140

*At the Concert* ...................................142

*Of Conventions ... and Cotton Candy* ................144

*Waiting to Serve* .................................146

*...Sist...Sist...Sister, Pick Me!* ........................148

*Confessional Poem:
May God Strike You Dead!* .......................154

*Of Course I Ate the Chocolate!* .....................161

*Lilacs and the Scent of My Mother* .................165

*For my mother,*
*who touched my soul*
*through her boundless love*
*for the written word.*

# Introduction

In your mind's eye, picture the last time you were moved to tears, or your heart broke, or your spirit soared, because of something you read that ignited passion within you. That's the power of poetry, **Touching the Soul**, breathing life and passion into your essence. Poetry is meant to be read aloud, whether in your head, or aloud to others. Poetry is meant to be acted out, each poem staged as a one act play, in, and of itself. And while it is true that not all poems stir the soul, those that actually do, are read, again, and again, and again! And embraced as priceless for generations!

My gift to you as reader, is to find a part of this book that touches your soul and embraces that connection! Whether it's the natural elements of earth, wind, and fire, that speak to you, **Taking Your Breath Away**, or the mysteries of **love**, or things **that hurt** when you read about them, it's about feeling those emotions. It could be **Challenging the Status Quo** and the fairness of life, or **Remembering  Place**, whether physical, or a state of mind, that touches your soul. ...Or it could be yearning for the good old days, **Waxing Nostalgic**. This poetry, dear reader, is **Simply for You**!

# Part I

# Taking Your Breath Away

# *Wake up the Dawn*

A peach stained sky saturates the darkness
On the Eastern horizon,
The sky begins to lift
Bleeding peach to pink streaks of color

The world awakens
To the acoustic exuberance
Of birds in flight,
Scorching the dawn
With small black silhouettes
Bouncing in the air...

Birds, creating vibrancy,
Creating drama for this fresh, new day

# Through the Looking Glass, Tableside

The stars are out,
Randomly tossed across a blank canvas
Playing well,
With everything that sizzles

Uncorking the night sky
Intimate and hushed,
Yet presented in a show stopping,
Pop-up adventure

Shooting stars
Dance between highs and lows
Playing to the universe below
Through the looking glass, tableside

# Two Gray Squirrels

Two gray squirrels squat
In the upper branches of a tall oak tree,
They loll in the sun
Splaying limbs and chatting with each other,
Sporadically, they sprint
And chew encrusted dead bark
Only to return to their squatting positions
Silently, taking pleasure in their world,
Their needs immediate and real,
Absurd in their simplicity

## Summer's Slide

The summer sky unmasks its artist eye,
Now renderings of shadows, bleak goodbyes
Its breathless ache unveils a secret wish,
Reversing autumn's hold for summer's bliss

.

## Autumn's Light

Adieu, adieu, the summer canvas fades,
Memories blur as crimson hues parade,
Skies screaming, orange burst of Autumn's light,
A harvest moon illuminates the night

## Autumn's Gift

A blitz of bright hues, yellow, orange, and speckled red,
Verdant hillside sprinkled with autumn's colored dust,
The master plan of spectacular vibrancy,
A leafy tribute to God's unconditional love
Ascending skyward, covering hillsides,
A bursting shock of brilliance, autumn's gift to us

## Autumn declares itself...

The sultry summer heat retreats
The sleepy pace steps up the beat
Orange and red tips stain the leaves
Another summer's slide, fading memories!

# Autumn Stomping

Coaxed to the ground by gusting gales
They lay in the gutter like colorful trails
Piled up to the curb in a random collection
Mayhem of mangled leaves needing added protection
From romping children dragging their feet
Crushing and crumbling their way down the street

Crush, mash, crush, mash
Crumble, crumble, crumble,
Happy children, stomping feet
The leaves all in a jumble

Crackle, crackle, creak...
Crunch, crunch, crunch...
A blaze of yellow and speckled reds,
Tangled in a bunch

It's crushing, crumbling, crushing,
Stomping little feet
Leaves are mashed into the ground
A happy, autumn treat

# Shooting Star

Cold water glistens, refracting white diamonds
Gobbled up and haplessly tossed across the sky,
*...of fading colors*
*...deceiving eyes*
*...and raging blackness,*
Dripping with pointed blinking
Of starry eyed wonders,
A shooting star flames across the sky
Shouting beginning and ending as one,
Instantly transfixing mere mortals,
Coaxing eyes upward from the rootedness of dirt
To the infinite possibilities of forever!

# Falling Leaves

Leaves are falling, as falling they must.
Falling leaves from the trees, an autumnal gust
Swirling and swishing, swaying and swishing,
Swaying or swishing with gentle assists.

The breeze is rustling the leaves as they fall,
Sailing through air as they tumble, freefall
Swishing and sailing and blown by the wind
The blustery wind, which makes leaves bend and spin
Swirling and spinning, they lite on the ground,
First spinning, funneling, racing around.

Then singing they must...
They sing and they whistle
While twisting and swaying and swirling about
With reckless abandon, the leaves blow about

A wind that does usher and beckon the leaves
To sway and to swish and to fly in the breeze.
In haphazard patterns, they spin and swirl
While winds are a gusting to leaves in a trance

Dancing and prancing, and casting a spell
Then catching the gusts from the north winds as well
They limp and they gasp as they fall to the ground
And lay in the gutters without making a sound

The swish and sway and flailing about
And the help from the wind which is shouting out
All comes to an end as the leaves are laid out
For the next round of children who come crunching
about!

# Raking Leaves...

Bright foliage, colorful hues,
Yellow, yellow, mellow yellow, yellow, mellow yellow,
Orange which is partly yellow and streaked with orange fire,
Where fire is bright and leaves a fright
And crackling and crackling,
And spitting and crackling and waiting in pile of leaves!

The sounds of leaves which are *raked and raked,*
*raked and raked,*
*And raked--*
Raking, raking, scraping and raking
And raking and scraping it goes!

Taking a break with piles left to rake
For a job which is never done,
For the fall leaves are falling
The falling of leaves,
They fall and fall and fall,
In need of scraping and raking and raking
and scraping again--
And again and again and again!

The circle continues as raking is taking a long,
long time to tend,
The circle continues, the patterns arranged
But falling leaves cover the trails with a rage
The winds they do blow,
They blow leaves from the trees
And falling leaves cover, so the grass we can't see!

So back to the raking and scraping and raking some more,
Keep raking and scraping and breaking at four
For nature is clever and holds all the cards
So one must keep raking and scraping their yards!

Persistence pays off with sore muscles and joints,
Fall leaves will return
I ask, "What's the point?"
Put down the raking and scraping and jump into the leaves,
Have fun in the yard and enjoy the leaves as you please!

## Sky Screen

Streaming white tails
Streak through azure blue skies, creating *skyscapes...*
Creating a  billowing explosion
*...of eroding artwork*

Jets coordinate to form artificial cloudscapes
Where man and nature converge,
A rolling surge of ever changing drama,
An artist eye upon a blank sky screen.

# A Flower Grows

A flower grows from seeds beneath the ground
With help from sun and toil from human hands,
It brings great pleasure, a burst of color found
For all to see, unfolding color grand

## Cracking Dawn

The light awakens me before five
The birds begin with a single fluted call
I listen to the wobbling of competing birds
Seeming intent on living life to the fullest

Nests in place, tucked in and safe...
Young birds squall for food
Necks out-stretched as if made of rubber,
The longest day of the year begins
Teeming with the incessant chatter
Of a thousand birds cackling

I listen to the beating of wings
Flitting birds lite on a tightrope,
        *...Stenciled into the rising sun*
        *...Cracking dawn*

## Summer Sunset

The summer sun retreats.
A painted sky reveals itself, enticing lovers all
To linger, stretch out upon the sugar sand
The sunset loudly proclaims itself a colorful umbrella,
Cloaking secrets of passion, climaxing under sunset skies

A mixture of perfume and sweet suntan oil
Co-mingle under pastel ribbons of color
Where bodies collide with streaks of orange fire,
Merging both, in sync

# Eating Ice Cream

Luscious, creamy, brain freeze electrifying,
Cooling temperatures on a hot summers night.
My tongue, swirls in streaks, circling round and round
the cone
Injecting warm tongue into sweet ecstasy!

A minty flavor snares my nostrils sweet,
Teeth grinding into chocolate chips
       *...over and over,*
       *... up and down*
All senses heightened, lips and tongue engaged,
Eating ice cream, on a warm summer's  night!

# FOG...

Quietly!  At first in patches, floating swiftly towards
shore,
The fog, all powerful, gathers without warning—
*engulfing, obliterating,*
A white-out, void of time and space,
All things disoriented, unable to see, rendered helpless

...**But then**, Fog sits quietly, embracing me, wet and sweet,
Coating the shore with silent resolve
A *perfect* lover, understanding and soft,
It echoes the cries of sounds within its gentle embrace,
And then, *detaching,* moves on.

# Stillness in the Georgian Valley

I.

The sun slowly rises
Filling the valley
With puddles of liquid sunshine
A resolute silence
Bores its way into the morning light
Stillness,
The Soul of this place
Soft, sweet, utterly Zen

II.

Silence pours itself deep within
The crevices of this valley
Creating a canvas
Upon which stick figured trees
Tall and lanky
Hold firm,
Pencil sketched into the landscape,
Branches steely and randomized,
A million lacy tendrils
Splayed across a landscape
Creating a Still-life

# Liquid Sunshine...

Liquid sunshine, hazy gray, peeking sunlight
Umbrellas carried in anticipation
A carousel of colors waiting to unfurl
A moment of sunlight, expectations raised--
Quickly dashed by liquid sunshine,
Splashes of sunshine upset by dark shadows
Marching orders...

> *...Rain undoes*
>
> *... the Spirit*

*Time and again, the land of eternal winter!*

## I Will Go Walking

*Uphill and downhill,*
Around and about,
Around and around, and around--
Trees on the left,
Trees on the right,
Trees so high, they cover the sky
As they *reach, reach, reach* for the stars in the night,
Starry and star-studded, and twinkling so bright

The trees stark, the wind does not blow,
As I *wind, wind, wind* up the mountain of snow.
Stretching and moaning, and groaning I go,
*Uphill and downhill*  to the valley below.
Silence envelopes me, sits in my ears,
Like radar, it catches everything that it hears,
Which is nothing, *no- thing* do I hear,
As I trudge up the hill...*again, and again and again!*

The pace is fast, but fast is not fast,
Rather slowly I climb, as the hills they go past.
The hills call my name, the birds chirp away,
As birds usually do
And I *climb and climb*
Until I hear two.

The music they make cuts the air like a knife,
And oodles of ducks join the chorus, bring life
The spell is unbroken as hills come and go,
My spirits are soaring out here in the snow
I trudge over hills– *up and down, up and down,*
Until my bones ache and my head it does pound
These hills carry me far away,
To one place, to my home in the hills

*Up hills and down hills,*
*I walk and I walk,*
*And I walk, and I walk, and I walk, and I walk, and I walk*
The peace that surrounds me is food for my soul,
And I will go walking until I am old
*Up hill and down hill,* and over again,
The rhythm of life,
*...And the power of Zen!*

## Enticing my senses

A warm breeze blows, *enticing* my senses …
To dream of far- away places,
I breathe the succulent nectar
Of places yet to explore
Untouched by time
Serenity, textured with layers of history
*My* adventure, *my* caverns of delight--
Isolated, yet familiar

# A Subtle Withdrawal

I stretch my toes, digging into wet, sugar sand
The water licks my toes
*Frothing bubbles...*
I squeeze my toes, curling them, thrusting sounds
*Back and forth...back and forth*
*Stretch... squeeze...stretch... squeeze*
Lapping waves retreat their course, *slowly*
A subtle withdrawal, laying bare my toes

# Night Falls

Night falls
The day's energy ebb,
The horizon pales
And the fat-bellied moon shines low in the sky

Stars slowly kindle the darkness
A peculiar calm unwinds
Within me
Familiar,
Tapping into Humanity's call–
Whispering to the silence of the night

# Veiled beauty

A swath of lace onto an iced windowpane
The transfer imperfect
A slightly decayed look upon elegance
Etching surfaces with a beguiling glow
While casting dark shadows,
Like black tempera paint.

# Part II

# In Love

# Wallowing in Could and Should

Could I love you more?
        Could I, Could I?
                ...Could, Could?
                        ...More, More?
                                ...or Should I love you more?
                                        Should I love you?
                                                Love you, love you more?
                                                        ...or less, or less??
                                                                Greater than, or More  than?

Could I, Could I?
        Not Should I, or Would I...
                Love you more, more?

If I Could, Could...
        Would, Would, Would love be stronger?
                If I Could, Could-- love you,
                        Would, Would I love you more?

Maybe, I Should, Should  love you less than!
        Would and Could demand more of the heart...
                and less of Should
                        for Should, Should implies neediness!
                                Where Could, Could opens possibilities
                                        ...and where long lasting love Would follow.

                                ...Should, Should I love you?

# Ping-Ping!!

I carry your voice in my head
The gentle click, click, clicking
Strumming away on my phone,
No discernible pattern evident

*Ping, ping*:  I love you!
*Ping, ping*: Don't you love the closeness
The deliciousness
Of *this* moment?

Pendulating, waning...
Vanishing words
Setting up the *zig*,
Waiting for the *zag*...
The bubble of green
...or blue
Flashing like a ping pong ball
In the volley of our lives

*Ping, ping*:  Just moved left
*Ping, ping*:  Coming back the other way
*Ping, ping*:  The white screen punctured
Waxing brighter,
Seeming to float a mile or two away
Ping, ping:   In the moment... that's enough
Ping, ping:   A rainbow of color volleying back and forth
Ping, ping:   ...or a mirage?

Wishing you home,
Click, click, clicking my red shoes
In hopes of seeing you
Ping, ping:  But in the meantime
*...Hearing your voice,*
*...Smelling you,*
*...And tasting every word*

# Barricade Stormer

Over tops of pointed thorns daring victory
Beyond mistakes by strangers waiting in shadows
Not just lives of people but of tossed away odds and ends
Hoarded as raw material in fruitful disarray
No holding back on life,
Pure poetry and performance together
In a floor to ceiling environment called "life"
Destined to reinvent self as participant
Slyly ironic, never quite knowing how sublimation plays out
Bringing a new paradigm as vision for the future
Wearing his soul on his sleeve!

# Complicated

A tangled web of relationships
Patterns of long ago...
That seemed certain and clear

Overlapping layers
Long forgotten except for ...
Scattered Kodak memories

Life, marching lockstep in a steady cadence
Constructing new realities
Blurring past nostalgia of home and hearth at Christmas
Crystallizing a new reality,
A new snapshot of life in progress
The past, creating a complicated separation of reality
For a generation gone by

# Searching...

If you could run away,
Would you?
Would you run away?
Would you, would you?
Could you, could you run?
Run, run away as far as you could or would?
A run away!

What would I do if you could, could, could run away?
My run away!
Would I follow you?
Or would you lead me?

Would I wander aimlessly searching for you?
Would I?
I would, would!
Would I be successful in finding you?
Or would my heart break each time I called your name?
...Sob, sob, sob, sobbing
...Cry, cry, cry, crying
..Scream, scream, scream, screaming...

Outwardly, physically distressed

And screaming your name
Commanding you to listen, to come to me
Inwardly, I match those screams, those screams
igniting inside!

Trembling with fear
as I call, call out,
Scream, and call out your name
Helplessly,
Hoarse with anticipation

Should I, should I stop searching for you?
Now that I have wandered
...up and down,
...down and up,
...over and under,
...inside and outside
...above and beneath...

Helplessly,
Haphazardly,
Systematically,
Defying all sensibilities!

Searching for you
Finding nothing

NO thing
A vacuum

No time for despair
or is there?
After such fright?
...Such searching,
...Such wrenching pain!

Of reckless abandonment
This wandering and calling out
These shoulds...
These stops and starts!

And then...
You appear
BUT even now I must
...cajole you,
...coax you,
...coddle you
Into turning around and facing me...FACE ME!

# Valentine's Day

*Red, red, red, red!*
*Brilliant red, sturdy red, brilliant sturdy red, blood red!*
*A dozen red, happy dozen, full of life dozen, the color red,*
*red, red!*
*Purposefully imposing red, and with lasting power,*
*deepening in its redness, circling and vying for attention...*
*More red, brighter red, see-me red, see-me symbols of love,*
*red love...*
*Cozy, long lasting love...*
*Never before love, love, love...*
*Dedicated love, somber love, complete with baby's breath*
*love...*
*Surrounding and crowded love, red, red, choking red...*
*Red, red, surprisingly low priced red, low priced and*
*crowded...*
*Choking river red, a circle of red, baby's breath, bound*
*tightly!*
*...an oxymoron for love*

# Nameless at the Landings Bar

The early fall envelops
Darkness whispers to the night
From the depths of lost souls wandering
Lurking shadows out of sight

Invisible pheromones stirring up hope
For all the nameless people trying to cope
Sharing a moment suspended in time
Shuttering the loneliness, and the nine to five grind

# A Prisoner Affixed

Flirtatious, loud, seductive…
Gentle waves caress my body, hugging me
My chair directed upon the sand
Until ever so slowly,
The lapping waves creep closer, no warning
Forcing me down, restraining me
Sucking me into its soft, supple core,
*Wet sand…*
Immobilized into wet sand
My chair slips salaciously down under
*…A prisoner, affixed to sand*

# Without Like...

Love, Love, Love,
Without Like
does not endure
but turns to lust
...Or love lost or lost love

Love without possibilities
Without possibilities...
Without on and on, and on
...Or off and off and off
Without like.

Like *changes* love,
Illuminates love,
Transforms love--
When like is likely.

A lifetime of tomorrows,
...of friendship,
...of connecting
...of comfortable walks on the beach

Like is _like_ this
...or that
...or here and there
Of like... and life... and love
Where love *is* liking
Intertwined, entwined
And like is love
And love then lasts
And lasting is forever...
As love is!!!

# Pub Talk

Languages blended, a cacophony of laughter
Entwined, interwoven as though there were no barriers
A comforting roar of non-denominational sounds
Rising, lowering, uniting as one voice
Diversity alive, screaming to be heard
Pardoning the world from unspeakable wrongs
Delivered in the name of country,
        One voice,
        One right,
Instead, in this one place, at night, in a pub
Many voices proclaim love, laughter
No hidden agenda!

# Part III

# And It Hurts

## I WEEP

A single teardrop, grim,
An acid irritant,
Tortured within its vapors,
Reflections of a thousand helpless children
Weeping,
Convulsing,
Gritty reminders of a vision affected
By senseless wars,
Triggered by anger and remorse,
Rotting corpses devouring their prey
Pretending to weep while luring children,
Common consequences of war,

A single tear- stained message
Provoking irritation,
An insincere display of grief
And dishonest remorse,
Sobbing sounds locked within a single tear,
This despicable treatment of children,
Shedding this tear,
This acrimonious tear,
A single manifestation of a menacing world
**Trickling down the cheeks of humanity.**

# Lollipops

Lollipops in the midst of grief
Where small talk has epic meanings
New ways to relive childhood
All manner of delicious excess
Countless hours of hoping
That something happens
Repressed, rambunctious
A common thread
Weaving together disparate lives
Of childhood, lollipops, and
Grieving

# Womb Raiders

Rolling, thunderous,
Undulating sounds that swirl and bite the way a
snake does
before the transference of distressed milky womb
layers of muted cobwebs
decaying in corners without translucence,
baring the carcass of living intent disturbed
by layers spread out on soft sand unfolding in ripples

Stirrings of sweet milk trapped, fouled by tethering
and suppression
into the clouds, dark, unfolding blue gray,
Spreading thighs, igniting and creeping between
sheets of storm clouds,
Baiting itself and swelling from sweat of ashen
tincture
*...blown away but not forgotten*

# Forgiveness

Smooth velvet colors of purple and soul,
Crystalizing imprints
Stripping shellac and filling cracks,
Caustic erosion of searing heat,
Erratic pumping of creamy sludge from pores and orifices
Releasing breath--to touch the scorching sun
Where unicorns fly, casting butterflies on wings and
Gentle stirrings of creation,
Before ants, before flies, before rodents, before the sun,
Releasing the presence of purity,
The sensuality of peace warming,
The destiny of forgiveness

## Surrender

Withered, distilled to nothing
A pulse barely worthy of candlelight
Wicks dancing like Ballerinas,  twisting and turning
Alive in the burning glow
Now stepping treacherously, flopping down
Into the pale yellow stillness of the edges of life,
A moth with wings impinged
Delaying the inevitable,
Disarray, jumbled notes upon a jar, imprecise and clumsy,
Staggering princesses, devining that  their princes save them,
An undeclared holiday from stifling numbness,
Withered limbs snuffed out by gentle breeze

## Too Busy to Notice

Straining to unleash the world's burden,
An elephant stomping lightly
Inflicting an unseen and unfelt presence
Flitting, like a moth attracted to a burning light
Wings singed and burning, no time to fall
Fire of wings carrying scars of a lifetime
*...Of wanting to dance on Dancing with the Stars*
*...Of wanting to feel alive like the adventurers on Survivor*

*Instead,*
Rumblings on a stage, eyes forward
And rolling back to avoid contact
Flashes of insight like pollinated flowers content
And crazy mosquitos, bites that itch and bleed untended
Grotesque and disfigured
*No time for fireflies, and jars, and romps through fields*

# Relic Fragile Now

A smorgasbord of early tastes and obsessions
Embodied in small scale objects
Preserved in -tact
And created from scratch
Elitist snobbery
Everything  larger, grander, grosser
Deceptions, contradictions
Empty ethical calories
Transported to window-shops and dumped
And versions of itself mirrored and encased to form right angles,
Pleasing everybody but going nowhere

# Disconnecting

A slight touch of the hand
Light, tingling,
Like a grain of sand upon a beach,
Like a never ending tide stretching out, playing to edges of
frothy shore
And crapping birds,
Like a star studded night soon blanketed by clouds
By penetrating fog, torrential rainfall
Like a groan of boats straining
To avert obliteration, of all connections from night to sand–
Disconnecting, disengaging life, blinds down
Coded in signals indiscernible
Entangled in a wretched stew of decomposition and
acceptance

# Forbidden

Blinded by wrestling touch on all sides,
Stiffening limbs parting
Drinking in the toxic liquid of *him*
Pumping fast to the heat of passion
Breath uneven, contemplating a picture of a different kind
His actions confusing,
The gentle caress, the exaggerated importance to every
syllable uttered
Every movement a calculated risk, hypersensitive to his touch
Her, depressed rather than soothed, organically deluded
By thoughts of him, an onslaught of conundrums
Expressions of a love forbidden

# Beaten

*(meant to be read aloud...in a sing-song pace. The poem depicts man beaten down and resigned.)*

**He sits and sits**– and sits, and then stands and sits and stands, and walks on command – when prodded and poked, and poked and poked, and prodded with fingers and hands.

The hands command the sits and starts, and starts and sits and stands, while strutting faster and slower and slower and faster, a marionette pulled and prodded, and prodded and pulled, and dancing in circles– while strutting and sitting and standing.

The voice drones on, and on and on– in circles, of droning and moaning, in a baritone drone, while droning and droning, and moaning and droning, in undulating waves, of boring and snoring, and groaning and moaning, while prancing and dancing, and sitting and standing– *go on*– *and on*– *and on*– *and on*– *beyond*–

# Vulgarity's Abrasive Master

Self-deprecating and willfully tasteless,
Narrow eyes grow even narrower,
He cackles gruffly
Burying face into sweaty palms

Ashamed, rendered speechless,
Summoning strength,
Lowering gaze,
A bundle of tics and peccadilloes

Picturing her in a way he would recognize,
Sorry to part ways and teary-eyed

A conundrum of gently missing you
And Frankenstein turned Wolf Man,
Making no sense whatsoever--
*Scolding and laughing at the same time*

A stream of conscious riffs
And a running commentary
Deluding the world's perception of him
Vulgarity's abrasive master

# Mental Break-down...

The darkness intensifies the confusion,
A combination
Of silence and darkness
Visual hallucinations

12" concrete walls
All sounds filtered
Too faint for the human ear
Ambient noise, negative decibels

In a darkened chamber
No startling sounds
A pristine environment
Utter silence

No humming of reassurance
Acutely aware of one's own bodily functions
*...heart beating,*
*...lungs filling,*
*...stomach gurgling loudly,*
**Punctuated by nothing**

# Divisible

Life, seeping from withered womb
Carrying searing pain,
Replete with images of angels,
*...On and on and on*, strapped and shackled

The stalwart enemy pursued
Through mechanical blowing of trumpets,
Patiently,
Touching complex creases of time

Learning through experimentation,
Bendable in geometric, folding sensations
Molding shattered glass,
Zigzagging through peaks and valleys

Tearing at sections of life through centuries,
...Of patterns embedded infinitely
Gently wacked and released
Caring less about labels
And pushing the limits of perfection within

# Ravages of War

Clinging to dwellings,
Funerals in a staggering war,
Guilt- ridden weddings
Under harrowing circumstances,
Hope imminent

*But soon...*
Resignation pushes sadness
Crying out in response to gunfire,
Rapid change,
Moments of happiness upended...
 *...Despair*

# Cruelty of Time

Time erodes the ashen shades of colic.
A pall of hanging embers–
Clings to cloth
*Remorse–*

Cracked sphere measuring crystals
Arranged in mangled mazes
Hanging charred
Imbued with death's lasting peace

# Is Anybody Out There?

## I.

Is anybody out there?
Does anybody care?
Fraught with disappointment
Riddled with despair
Hoping for a lifeline
Tossed out in troubled seas
Betting on illusions
That is their destiny
Too many people lonely
Adrift on silent seas
Afraid to chart their own course
They risk their destiny
Why can't the lonely people rush out to helping hands
To guide them through rough waters
And rough and tumbled lands
Is anybody out there?
Does anybody care?
I do. I do.

## II.

I was that lonely person
Who reached for helping hands
The churning waters rising
To cover supple sand
A lifeline in the waters
Encircled me with love
The searing pain subsided
The time to heal is now
I will be there to guide you
To help you chart your path
Traversing troubled waters
Finding love at last
I will.  I will.

# A Free-Wheeling Life...

Weaving in and out of traffic,
A free-wheeling life
On two wheels,
Two Big City wheels
Constantly moving
To avoid wagging fingers
And judgmental fools

Slick and sweet!
No shame, no blame!

A free-wheeling life
Mudguards and all,
Gliding over long straights,
Tough choices deferred

Flying over steep speed bumps,
Edgy, aggressive,
A free-wheeling life
Flying high before the ultimate fall!

# Part IV

# Challenging the Status Quo

# "The Stir"

Gatherings, meet-ups,
Large scale happy hours!
Online matchmakers entice
with a new level of dating,
*...Make fresh pasta*
*...Go on hikes*
Pheromones and human nature
*...Converge*

No more personal chemistry
using statistical science or personality quizzes
*Instead*, create dating opportunities
the old fashioned way
Singles' parties,
Crowded together--
*Lip to lip*
Consuming alcohol and flirting

*"The Stir"* acting as a filter
Back to basics...
Meeting in a bar...
Low tech style...
*Stirring up* relationships
*The old-fashioned way!*

# In Sync ...

When life's in sync, happiness echoes back,
Vibrations resonate, steady, strong
Awakening the spirit
Heralding  peace and solitude

When life's in sync, happiness echoes back,
Reverberating-- strings of harmony
Playing out life's dreams
*No room for fallen angels*

When life's in sync, happiness echoes back,
An easy target for unscrupulous thieves
Disequilibrium, rhythms unhinged
*For a moment fallen angels prevail*

But, when life's in sync, the rhythm of life resumes,
Not silently, nor patiently, but loudly
Proclaiming happiness, no pretenses
Happiness echoes back
All's right with the world!

# Boxes of Wishes

Small-town people, media fed
Caricatures of a middle class
Barely competent enough to manage ordinary human
interactions
And comforted with tears and disturbing confessions

Bullies in a foul mouthed imagination
Boxes of wishes created
And served up by obnoxious, hysterical Narcissists!
Duped!

# Unfolding Regret

Coffee served up again and again
The ritual morphs from welcome to avoidance
An affair relegated to a low social level
Each coming to grips with the loss

A blank performance subject to interpretation
A somber domestic drama of unfolding regrets
Some of the set ups cringe- inducing,
Looking for substance but disenfranchised

# Dark Demons Within

*Exploiting the problems of poverty and corruption*
*To gain support,*
*A miserable pretext of Patriotism*
*With devastating consequences*

*A massive surge raging against the middle,*
*Worrisome at best,*
*Hurled against the fabric of Democracy*
*Perverting a system meant to serve us all,*
*Now, held hostage*
*To a new Master*

*A veritable make or break moment,*
*No appearance of impropriety,*
*Timing is everything*
*Extremists once licking the fringes*
*Now stirring the boiling pot*
*Dark demons within, at war with democracy*

# Ordinary People Crushed

Mellowed by time and influenced by hazy memory
*Ordinary, decent people*, cry out, without a voice
For a time long ago, or so they say...

When people were kinder, politics more gentile
And people lived off the earth
Not on the edge of a precipice,
*Ordinary people*, from a culture of extraordinary endurance,
Mustering up courage, to endure yet another day,
*Ordinary people*, steely- nerved,
Now, heartbreaking encounters with bleak destinies,
Home and hearth destroyed by *American Greed*,
Home foreclosures– the norm!

Older, more somber people, dazed by the lightning speed of their lives torn asunder,
Dignity stripped away, destitute and raw
Wondering how *this* "Recession" could have taken hold in a country into which they submitted themselves body and soul, wrapped in patriotism,
Unflagging resolve to serve.

Mere children smelling of the filth of a war decades
into and yet still unjust,
A war living off the backs of *Ordinary people*,
thriving on the backs and limbs of *Ordinary people*
Content, as wars can be, to whisper the chilling truth
and cast doubt on its authenticity as young men and
women traverse this Land of Plenty–
homeless, limbless, numbed, and bewildered.

*Ordinary people* adrift in a land fertile tended to–
for *over* 200 years,
Now stripped of everything: dignity, money, basic
rights, *yet still pretending*–
That this America still stands for its people,
still stands for all that is noble in its constitution,
still stands for the symbol of freedom.

Duped, stupefied, and defeated,
*Ordinary people* shamed, humiliated by the
*Greed Makers* who cast them from their homes,
And pumped them full of drugs as they aged,
And sold them the "God Bless America" s***!

# Fading Wish

Cinematically perfect,
Revolving magical views reaching out,
Tussled by a growing brood of a thousand peasants,
Pawns in a vast global chain

A legacy
Replaced by divine intervention
And transforming the landscape
Of humanity

Where grandchildren are fed and clothed for school
And starving,
Eking out a meager existence

A magical view diminished,
A fading wish,
Saving a rainbow--
May be too late

# Undo the Did? Never!

*(Poem MUST be read aloud to be appreciated fully!
...or GO HOME!)*

I like what I did, when I did, what I did!
I will do what I did –did/ da- do/ da-da did/
Da- did- did/ da-did/ do- did /did- do/
Do/ do/ do-do/ do/
Did/ did/ da- did/

What's did is done/ da-da/ da-da/ done/
Done/ done/ do-done/
Da-da/ da-da/ done/
Undo what is done?  No/ no/ NO-NO can do!

Da- do/ do-do- do/undo/ do- da-do/ do/
No can do! I like what I did!
Do- did/ da- did/ da- do-do/ da-do/
I'm done with what I did-do/ did/da-did/ do/

***...GO HOME!***

# Ugly Sheep

**(A parody about prejudice and discrimination)**

It was mentioned in a most apologetic way.
*This* was the field of ugly sheep, black sheep and all.
The field opposite a bed and breakfast
On which a handful of ugly sheep gathered, trying to fit in.

Ugly sheep, big creatures, long legs, long bodies, long necks
Some with bare skin, carrying a blueness about the face
and legs
Replete with Roman noses.
And then there were *those* big ears, more like a donkey
than a sheep,
*Really!!*

There were also black and white ones,
dotting the landscape,
The black ones considered taboo,
Hiding out far from view
Unable to contend with the ridicule,
Hugging tight to the wall, with backs up,
Erect ears like radar, ensuring their own safety,
From afar, resembling speckled black dirt
*Most* unappetizing

In some places country farmers cull–
And report ugly sheep in their flocks
...*"Xtreme sheep"*
Undesirable wool features:
Uneven wool; bare patches; worse, no wool at all;
or highly rubbery and wrinkled skin
Culled by farmers
Random genetic mistakes,
Sticking out like sore thumbs

Whatever will become of ugly sheep?
Is it possible to let the "ugly" ones live in the world?
Rather than face ridicule and elimination?
Fortunately, they have since been moved
*It was all for the best!*

# Collision of Worlds (Ferro painting)

**Spheres...**
>Suspended in time and space,
>Floating to, or from nowhere
>...or somewhere, or somehow
>A collision of worlds
>
>Life seeps, appears, disappears from cracked sphere,
>Cracked not crushed
>Never crushed,
>But suspended, separated, cracked sphere

**Floating spheres...**
>Toward suspension of reality,
>Flirty and floating,
>And Flighty and floating,
>Fragile, not crushable
>But fragile in flight,
>Flirty in flight
>
>Never–never land—bound
>Floating by, yes bye,
>By-the-by
>End of time by

Where space collides
And time stands still,
As still, not standing still
But edging toward desire
Not passion

But where desiring passion is an arrow
And arrows break hearts,
Cracking and crushing

And time is suspended
And love is suspended

And life becomes a starry night
In the middle of the day,
...Not night
......But day
Suspended in time and space

# Kneading Bread

The staff of life,
Needing bread,
Kneading bread for those who need
Need, need, kneading bread

Working lovingly to make large vats of dough
For dough,
Bakeries, homes, all kneading bread
To anchor food

Floured hands massaging,
Using muscles, kneading bread,
Determining the outcome of bread
Before bread is baked

Compressing, pushing dough,
Heeling the dough
To heal a hunger within,
Healing dough,

Mixed in the right proportions–
And heeling, compressing, pushing, folding
And heeling, compressing
And pushing and folding over itself
–Again and again

*Heeling, pressing into the body*
*Forming a rhythmic motion,*
*Rhythmic, musical,*
*Compressing, smoothing, folding*
*Compressing, smoothing, folding*

*Satiny,*
*A sheen forms,*
*A smooth, silky sheen*
*Creating doneness,*
*Bread which is done, done, done*

*Pressed with fingers,*
*Sometimes benched and shaped again*
*But stretched, stretched, stretched without breaking*
*Until smooth and silky,*
*Silky and done*

*Kneading bread,*
*Compressed and pounded and prodded*
*Into smooth and silky,*
*Done!*

*Kneaded enough*
*And enough needed for all,*
*Doneness, well done,*
*The staff of life,*
*Kneaded well, for people in need*

# New England Giant Pumpkin Weigh-In (at the Topsfield Fair)

Start with a seed, a proven champion winner,
Give it time and water, and cater to its every whimper,
The yearly quest to grow a two ton pumpkin for the
Topsfield fair,
Will the record be broken, or does anyone really care?

The stakes are high for these competitive growers,
The money and the prestige will be heightened or lowered,
Keep the size secret for there is always quite the fight
To win the freakish pumpkin contest on which they've
set their sights!

Avid New England pumpkin growers on the great
pumpkin patch tour
Staring down the competition, keeping careful score,
In September pumpkins grow up to 30 pounds
or more a day
And pumpkin politics kicks in, as they close in
on the "weigh"!

Hefty big boys, a whopping 2,000 pounds
Large, fragile, lumpy, and sort of round,
Growing a giant orange pumpkin is a labor of love
At the mercy of luck and divine intervention from above!

## All That Matters...

Insulated, fragile–
Held together by wire and tape, and injections into flesh,
to keep away demons that would rob them of this moment

Pigskin flesh, *all that matters*
Tossed about as sacred,
Cornered and cradled as a baby Jesus in wanton arms
Pigskin, yearning to be embraced

Warriors,
Ignoring the cost to flesh or future remembering
For the glory of this moment,
A euphoric feeling of immortality,
Soaring on wings of crushing explosions
Falling silently, convulsed and broken on the battlefield

Coaxed into scoring
By the deafening roar of chanting fans,
Hungering for carnage in a vile arena
Where warriors soar effortlessly in acrobatic splendor,
And egos are forgotten at the moment of collision

*Nothing mattering but intensity and guts–*
*Formidable opponents*

# What's All the Fuss About?

*The Dark Knight Rises*, a movie, showing at midnight
In Aurora, Colorado in July.

A dark knight "appears"
Out of nowhere,
Part of the action adventure?
Dressed the part

This piece of the movie
*Fitting in*,
A sinister, holographic character
Designed to enhance a movie "event" such as this?
*...or a tragedy unfolding?*

What's a movie goer to think?
Part of the ambience of today's movie experience?—
*Possibly!*
Part of the scene unfolding on the "big screen"?—
*Possibly!*

...Or part of the cultural drama
      Unraveling in America
            Reminding Americans of the violence
            routinely embraced
            ...in far away wars
            ...in virtual gaming, 21st century style
            ...in real life

Just push the reset button
All is forgotten
A "virtual" clean slate
Start over!

**What's the fuss all about?**

Second chances for breaking the score
"Racking up" points
Victimizing, vaporizing all opponents,
Second chances to "keep on, keeping on"
Game on...

**What's all the fuss about?**

*The Dark Knight*, a thriller,
A block buster weekend
Thundering violence,
American culture imbued with
*This* form of entertainment,
Inoculated against violence

### *What's all the fuss about?*

Children, mere babes
Attending the midnight screening,
Children, warriors of violence,
Anointed with violence,
Both on and off screen
A witness to their own vulnerability
Much too early

### *What's all the fuss about?*

All tactical materials available freely,
Legally
On the Internet,
Just plug in your credit card number!
Good to go!

### *What's all the fuss about?*

Spraying theater goers
Using an assault rifle
Fed by high capacity magazines,
American is stunned!

*All* legal,
*All* in a "civilized" society,
*All* protected by our legislators,
Our Constitution
Cloaked in second amendment rights,
Solemnly cherished by the NRA

**What's all the fuss about?**

Be careful what you wish for–
*American Greed*, the winner,
*The American Dream,* on the losing side.—

# Stepping Out

Reaching the apogee of power,
Corruptions played over a grand stage
From deceptive tactics that confuse
Even the shrewdest

Unsubstantiated assertions going too far
Parroting preposterous thinking,
Flummoxed by the ticking clock,
Empty promises overrated-- *nothing comes from nothing!*

The absence of solutions for human needs--
An enemy of all mankind,
Ardent protesters
Unpracticed and out of sync

People from all walks of life
Lockstep, moving in new directions,
Daring to disturb the status quo
Taking a complex look at what it means to be human
*Stepping out!*

# Transformation

Turning strangers into friends with a quicksilver smile
Onscreen actions that create a fantasy world of
Artists and clanking pirates falling on a ship's deck,
Clarifying identity and breezing past bold assumptions
Like a curvaceous silver pussy cat on the prowl
Smugness and self- suspicion
Turning friends on haunches like feral cats

# YOLO, YOLO

*(You Only Live Once—meant to be read aloud in a sing-song fashion)*

**YO, YO, YO– LO, LO, LO– YOLO, YOLO, YOLO– LO**
**YOLO** to the max, as max, as max does max
On the top of the heap, **YOLO, YOLO**
Rapping **YOLO, YOLO**– You Only Live Once!
**YOLO, YOLO, RAPPING YO, YO, LO, LO, LO**
Everyday, everyday, rapping **YOLO, YOLO**
**YO, YO– LO, LO, LO**, Rap, Rap, Rap
RAPPER DRAKE RAPPING– RAP ON, RAP ON –
WITH **YO** MOTTO– **YOLO**
Only youth kicks out the MOTTO, **YOLO, YOLO**,
Kicking hi, kicking low, **YOLO, YOLO**, You Only Live Once

You Only Live Once, as once may be too much
Or once in a lifetime, or anyone's lifetime
The craze foolhardy, a foolhardy craze,
Carpe diem, carpe diem!
Tote cray-cray– tote, tote, cray-cray
Live the day!  Youth carefree, carefree living, without fear,
Or consequences for tomorrow a little too near,
**YOLO, YOLO**– *HEY, HEY-HEY– HEY, HEY*, **YOLO, YOLO!**

# Dissolving Boundaries

Boundaries dissolve between self and nature
Leaving urban worlds behind
...for castles and transformations
Taking place in trees and sky,
Elements of self,
*Breathe life*

Recklessness that feels refreshing
A reminder that fireflies
Float up and envelop,
Pulling back,
Awakening promises of dissolving boundaries

## Be still, the Lie

Diamonds of hope, dancing on aquamarine,
Sunrise heralds another day in paradise!
Silently, demons *skulk* still waters
Black and dead, creamy sludge-- *Be still, the lie.*

# Blurred Vision

No need for a noble cause to energize the masses,
Mediocrity will do
Alter dynamics without losing identity,
Wistful but naïve, *blurred vision!*

New reasons to rant, cookie-cutter characters the
norm,
Frustrations running high
Climbing steadily with a spate of attacks
Viral outrage, *blurred vision!*

Profoundly fragile personalities,
Fevered believers who populate the fringe
Handling absurdity,
The genesis of their indignity, *blurred vision!*

*Striding upright,*
*Fully involved,*
*Fully caffeinated*
The bubbly outrage flattened,  *blurred vision!*

# Wandering toward Nothingness...

**Maybe** there is order to the way things order be.
Or **maybe, maybe the maybe** of the order,
should be apparent if eggplant were the order of the day
of which day there are many who are deemed
as wandering toward nothingness.
Nothingness, nothingness abounds in that great order
of the universe that presents itself
as food for thought, or thought of as food, or not food at all
in spite of itself. **Maybe!**

# Struggling for the Right Fit

Part of the evolution of etiquette,
Creating new norms
And nurturing relationships through digital natives
To find balance,

Screaming,
Decreasing amounts of tolerance
For unnecessary communication,
A burden and a cost

Snapping photos at 30 second intervals,
Switching off only when dark
Facedown,
Struggling for the right fit
While discounting strangers in a way that disconnects

Moving through spaces of differing sizes,
Afraid of miscommunication
Through walls being touch- enabled
**No off switch**
**No way to delete**

# Part V

# Remembering Place

# In the Underworld of Dust and Goo

Little Pooch wanders through cracks and crevices
*Unseen-*
Content under the bed,
Co-mingling with the oddball sock and stray pencil

Master over, snug in a warm bed listening to chimes
of ancient clocks
Pooch snuggled into his own tight ball of soft cotton
beneath,
Only snuffling sounds emit to puncture the cracking
 of dawn
*...Master up*
*...Pooch under*
In the forgotten underworld of dust and goo
Waiting for that precise moment
When both arise,

Sounds of a door squeaking to life
Slowly herald a break,
A quarter turn of the doorknob signals escape is near
Then, Pooch cleverly disappears into the daybreak.

## Two Perspectives:

## Sail Away (Light)

Sail away with me
Through the setting sun
Into the soft night
Mainsail bulging
Like a fat bellied moon
Bathed in constellations, telling tales

Sail away with me
Blanketed by shimmering stars
Reflecting back a million twinkling diamonds
Randomly colliding
Splintering the sea

Sail away with me
Gliding silently under full sail
Caressed by night winds whispering
And cloaked in the silent night

*What will be, will be—*

# Sail Away (Dark)

Bleeding trails, streaking the setting sun
Casting darkened embers toward the sea,
The reality of escape
Telltale ruins
Of an unfulfilled life
Shedding tears of past reflections

A million regrets
Repenting and hopeless
Like a tumorous aching unleashed
And echoing the cold, disaffected, black sea
*...Searing pain*
*...Numbness*
A sterile existence
Sail away,

*What will be, will be!*

# Friendship's Gift

Sleeves pulled inside out...
Contents raw
Laying bare clothes and heartaches
Like pennies on a street
Overlooked, stepped over
A tarnished piece of copper
Turned heads up
Facing cold elements of weather
Worthy, mighty, yet passed by

*Except by friends...*
Noticed and accepted, tarnish and all
Picked up, savored up, but never held up
To ridicule,
Polished with *Bon Ami*, less abrasive, gently coaxed
To life
Until tears are washed away
Until whatever time it takes to listen
Dancing on moonlight and playing out dreams,
Friendship's gift

# New England Rock Walls

Still rocks,
Silently carrying the burden of history
   *...of wars*
   *...of happy times*
Rocks, long ago tossed aside to make way
For fertile fields to flourish

Weathered surfaces,
Rock fabric--
Fine and coarse grain
Angular striations of minerals buried deep within
Glinting flecks of gold
Or strikes of silver,
Lichen covered stones
Building character along with age

Timelines of history
These rambling rock walls
*...Deepening appreciation*
*...Connecting generations*
A New England rock wall,
A unique timepiece
By which to judge the passage of time

# Separating Boundaries

Rock walls,
Randomly textured cracks
Wandering aimlessly
Through small and large rocks

Creating confusion—
Yet, not,
Haphazardly arranged
Yet, making sense

Setting clear boundaries,
*...Separating lands*
*...Separating animals*
*...Keeping people out*

Wanting to comply
Duty bound to separate and divide
Yet, falling rocks over time
Stray from their assigned task

*Rock walls,*
*Bound by rocks*
*Loosely piled*
*Yet, no boundaries*

*Loose rocks ,*
*Torn asunder by time*
*Naturally eroding man's efforts*
*To separate and disconnect*

# Stone Walls

Symbols of separation
Stone walls
Keeping at bay
Neighbors who feud
Bursts of anger
Proprietary squabbles averted

Stone walls
Stone on stone
Stokes of grey
Dark or light
Depending upon time of day
And thickness of surrounding woods

Stone walls
Still life,
Quiet, serene, calming
No agenda now
Symbols of separation
*...Long forgotten*

Stone walls,
Archeological ruins,
Nostalgic symbols
Of pastoral New England,
Now ornamental
But, instantly, authenticating history.

# A New England Sea Town

Pencil- like spires painted white,
Touch clouds
And sometimes merge
Rising above
Penetrating the skies
Dominating the landscape
The sentry, in a New England Sea Town
Cloaks and protects the jumble of buildings

A Sea Town, wedged between dark sea and skies,
Loose and sharp edged,
Folds of mustardy brown sand
And azure blue skies

Giant shards of flexed granite
Protrude from the sea,
Cool, jagged gray,
Steep and twisting,
And looping,
Mimic waves,
Stirring up the sea

Repetitions of a brooding soundtrack,
Waves swirl relentlessly
Against the 3-D still life landscape--
*Images of a rocky New England Sea Town*

# Yankee Farmers

Hardworking Yankee farmers
Building rock walls
To confine livestock,
Mark boundaries

Creating usefulness
From stone on stone
Lining roadways
From the land

Practical Yankee farmers
Building rock walls,
Platforms of stone
On which to build hearth and homes

Building rock walls on which to build barns
To contain and house livestock
High utility, versatility, ingenuity

Yankee farmers
Hardworking and practical
Building rock walls
...long ago

Yet, reaching through time,
Rock walls built by Yankee farmers,
Most now dismantled,
Reclaimed by forests long ago

A thousand stories to tell
*...A story of hard work*
*...A story of ingenuity*
*...A story of Yankee farmers*

# A Muted Shade of Motley Memories

*If*...Life were brighter shades of hues **if** shades were drawn, **if** hues and shades dimmed, **if** dimming shades were less bright, less of everything, but not less the less, the less of, but not including more of dimming less brightly than before, would the painting of my life be muted but not dimmed, or dimly muted, or muted but bright, brighter, brightest of the muting as, as, as, has muting dimmed the memories of the bright, brightly, mostly brightly felt, feelings of a bright light or rather dimmed, transcended into a muted shade of motley memories? Would, could shades mute, mute, mute the delectable tauntingly delightfully delectable memories of life, muted and all. *If...*

# Island Memories...

Unfurl the mast
*...Of multi-colored sails... of summers past,*
The crimson sunsets constrict the day
Edging out the frothy waves that rim the bay

*Memories...until next year!*

An island life, my summer dream
Surreal at times, my time serene
A pointillism... of blue hydrangeas
An island so friendly, there are no strangers
Only people I've yet to meet
Lining the benches along the cobbled stone street

Brandt Point lighthouse ushers the way
As the Steamship Authority docks at the bay
Memories treasured, trinkets abound
The island fades as I am homeward bound!

# Settling In

A peripatetic pace
Stoking a desire to establish solid roots,
Punctuated by summers with grandparents
in New England,
Comfortingly familiar

*Hungry,*
For the best life has to offer,
Indulgent upgrades
To classic traditions
Boosted by marshmallows and hot chocolate,
A wistful nod to home and hearth

One's place in a graceful community
*Shaping a life around an appreciation—*
*...Of old remembrances,*
*...Of new beginnings*

Breathing in steadfastly,
Wanderlust averted
Not settling for—
**But settling in!**

# A Lighthouse Stands

A lighthouse planted firmly in the sea
Its beam illuminating sailor's way to see
As danger lurks unseen, she stands her place,
The ships protected, beneath her warm embrace

# Tucked In—Nantucket

Tucked in tight
Proud, gray, shingled houses wait
Longing for summer

# ??? It is difficult to think of... ???

It is difficult to think of, hard to think of, critical to think of, thinking itself!

A thought happens, and happens as it may, continues to happen beyond what you thought would happen, as you find it important to happen-- of life and love.

Circling the thought, it transcends where it begins, sending the signal round in a circle of loving thought.

Thoughts which give or take, or hide, or make love or war, or this or that, depending upon which cologne you might be wearing, or might change your mind... or not need to wear any at all!

 In which case, the essence of the thought could or could not, or may or may not be influenced by memory, or not memory, or memory that relies on remembering which is not remembering-- if it cannot be remembered, while the thought itself— POOF! VANISH**ES!**

# Moving Boxes...

*(Must be read aloud playfully, with a swaying, moving motion, depicting the movement of boxes from one place to the next.)*

...boxes are moving as moving they must-- to move, or move, and move over hill and dale, and dale and hill, or hill or dale, nor hill nor dale, but ailing when moving, and moving when sailing, never giving or living, when moving or grooving, or dancing and sailing, and sailing and wailing, as boxes are moving over hill and dale.

...Crushed and smashed, and smashed and smashed, while moving and grooving, and proving and proving, that moving is rhythmic, and rhythmic is crushing, and crushing is smashing, while moving and grooving, not needing to prove– a thing!

...A thing which is moving and grooving, and proving and moving, and grooving over hill and dale. A thing, not nothing, but something which is nothing, still could it be nothing? ... if moving and grooving, and proving and moving, over hill and dale. Things and things, and things and rings, which bling and bling, when moving and grooving, and grooving and moving, and swaying to rhythmic sounds- - of crushing and smashing, and smashing, not grooving and moving, nor grooving, nor moving, but still...

...Still we continue to groove and move.  We move those boxes over hill and dale. Where dale is pale, and pale is ale, but not as yellow, or mellow, or mellow, or mellow, or yellow, or ready for tea at three.

With tea and me at three, and three and tea which is ready for me. And so it continues, over hill and dale, until moving is over, and tea is at three!

# Correspondence ON Simply Thanks!!!!!!

**Simply**, not complex, not difficult to understand, *not ever* so frilly, yet direct, so direct, ever so direct, directs *me* to accept *your* thanks, yet not really directing me, but divining me over and over and over and over, in such a sweet but not phony sweet, nor Stevia sweet, nor Equal sweet, nor the yellow stuff which no one can spell sweet. I accept *your* thanks with gratitude but not that humbly that it stifles, that it stifles, and it stifles me. Is stifles spelled incorrectly?? But I do not care, that it stifles my creativity and translates into inertia and laziness, and more laziness, until my toes are filled with such overwhelming laziness that it overwhelms me and makes me not care about anything... not my poetry, not my friends, not my family, not anything political, of which I want to care about caring. *Again, simply*, not in a complex way—***Thanks!!!***

# Bleak Misery

Trees planted firmly in the snow
Instantly violated by piercing winds
Winter committed to resuming its insurgence on the
night
Shutting down production of light in time for winter's
fight

Deeply wounding
Rising discontent
Life holed up together, negotiating the cold
Hammering out a compromise to the bitterness so
bold

Finally, emerging
To announce the birth of spring
Paving the way
For a desperately needed lifeline—
...*Spring!*

# Ancestral Sweeps...

At a precise moment in time,
Determined only by the ticking of my biological clock–
...*Edgar Allen Poe* style
A need,
Strong, burning,
Scattered with the aromas of a lifetime,
Washes over me
Beckoning me to reconstruct the footsteps
of my ancestors

Messy and turbulent– at times,
Lives intersect, closing in on me from all corners
of the world.
Ancestral sweeps, broad strokes
Each click of the mouse
Unlocks secrets tucked away
Leaping across time
From continents and oceans unfathomable,
Thirsty for more,
Never enough,

Hints through the time machine
Wanting the past to teach me
*...to lead me to my ancestral roots*
*...to turn back my biological clock*
Wondering whose womb cocooned each precious life
unearthed
Each life, unaware of the imprint made on the whole

I sit and breathe life into my past
*...Across time...Tick-tock*
*...A forward motion...Tick-tock*
*...Back to "then"...Tick tock*
For just a glimpse of something
That connects the beat of my heart to those here
before me,

A snapshot in time
Where all ticking ceases
And for just for a fleeting moment, time collides
With a life now
*...Reaching back,*
*...Breathing life,*
*...Reviving,*
*...Connecting generations*

The fragile beating of hearts
Intertwined through time
*As one...Tick-tock!*

# Dark Memories

Memories buried like gold
A jigsaw dismantled
Into a heap of broken- edged pieces
Moving backwards--*Into chaos*
Lacking a driving, unifying force
A dangerously splintered form
Fragmented and making little sense,
*Not* casually forgotten

# Dreamy

De-de-de-de-lish, lish, delish, delicious dream state
Dreamy, dreamily, dreaming dreamily,
Suspending time
Dreamily delicious,
Delusional, deluding reality,
Suspending reality,
Peachy, creamy, or creamy peach
Defying, defying, deftly defying,
…or lying by deftly defying reality
Delicious unreality, defying reality
De-de-de-defying reality--deliciously

# Something Lost Is Something Not Found

Something lost is something not found
Where finding is the surprise,
A wonder...wandering,
Ferreting out the find,
Picking up the find, the wonder of the find,
The delicious delirium of the find being found
About which is a loss no more,

A treasure, found to be infinitely more of the find
Than the find itself, exquisitely acting as if...
Not finding were not an option,
As if...the finding of the find, in and of itself,
 were the truest and most genuine find,
As if...not finding were not the option at all–
in the first place,
Only first place the option, the one and only option,
Something found, never lost but found
And treasured...the only option,
besides the find itself– of course!

# Part VI

# Waxing Nostalgic

# When All Is Still

When all is still...
The only sound,
The reassuring ticking of the clock
Reflecting back the sounds of life

When all is still...
A heartbeat, a steady cadence, a life line
Connects today's precious moments
With the collective heartbeats of a new tomorrow

Tomorrow, the connectedness to family
...*Auld lang syne*
Texting, tweeting, sweet sounds of family
Simple reassurances that life is eternal-
*For now...*

All the beats of a lifetime
All the tomorrows
Gather us together as one--
A million heartbeats
Gently cradled in the arms of time
When all is still

## Summer's Slide

The summer sky unmasks its artist eye
Now renderings of shadows, bleak goodbyes
Its breathless ache unveils a secret wish
Reversing autumn's hold for summer's bliss

# Nostalgia Reinvented

A turtle's pace, a nostalgic pastime
The movie theater drive-in, iconic
Cozied behind dashboards
The children play
To a shadow box screen
Before the movie ever begins!

The old fashioned drive-in,
Fragile business,
Sprawled on valuable farmlands
Merging shirtless youth
With famous movie stars
On a football sized digital screen

Artificial light combines with starry night
Like fireflies converging with constellations,
Smells and textures collide in a free- for- all
*Soupy cheese fries, part of the deal!*

Crackly speakers of old
Replaced by low frequency radio transmissions,
Late arriving cars, co-mingling with characters
On the giant screen,
And romance in the next car
Heats up the night,
More deserving of an "R" rating
*...Than the movie*

## The Clarity of Loss

Footprints, fading over time
Shallow imprints now
Obscured, unrecognizable
Transformative, dragging age behind in
dribs and drabs
Small blue birds, into hollow vacuums
Launching new ways to target loneliness
All trussed up to be the scapegoat
And declining to be identified
Repeatedly duplicating mistakes of loss
Seared and codified, encrusted
Imprisoned within a life of loss
Of missed opportunities crystallized–
The clarity of loss

# The Lady in Black

Hauntingly beautiful,
***The Lady in black–***
Exotic, ethereal, enchanting,
Floats along the grass dance floor
Effortlessly, in the moment

Head erect
Chiseled features
A statue come alive
Ballroom  style,
Wafting on clouds
As Beatle's music mesmerizes
On the soft summer night

Dancing carefree
***The Lady in black***
In a closely packed arena
Amid families,
Singing, laughing, dancing
No one notice
Yet everyone sees

### The Lady in Black
Arms raised, ballerina style,
Deftly, elegantly flowing
Gliding through the crowd
On gossamer wings
From one end to the other
Same step,
Same trancelike movements
Fluid and confident
No matter the song
A contrast to the piercing, simplistic Beatle's lyrics
A contrast in happenings

Long, thick, black hair
Loosely pinned,
Long tresses escaping
*As is she...*

Into a world all her own,
Inner peace, contentment,
Working the crowd
Yet lost in another time

No need for pretense
Yet creating her own pretense,
Performing
Ritualistic motions
Soothing, rhythmic,
Designed to hypnotize

A never ending dance
The sameness of step
Yet remaining true to the moment

Blending one Beatle's song into another
No matter—
***The Lady in Black***
Lifting her soul
To celebrate the '60's
*Namaste*

# Standing Here...

Standing here, on the edge
Of something big,
Something untried,
Reality strikes its mighty blow
Upending years, upon years, upon years, upon years–

Standing here, on the edge
Of something big,
Feeling it, intuitively
Understanding with certainty
*...of Robert Frost*
*...of The Road Less Traveled*
Understanding with uncertainty
Which one I will travel,
Does it make all the difference?
*...or not???*

Standing here, on the edge
Of something big,
Certain that either road traveled
Will lead to a comfortable life, a treasured life

But let's just think about it...or not?
Does either construct of reality really matter now?
*...just to me?*
*...just for me?*
*.. .just because of me?*

Standing here on the edge
Of something big,
Drumming its steady cadence
...wrenching into the depths of my soul

*On and on, on and on, on and on, on and on...*
*...Beyond the life well lived*
*...Beyond the expiration date of work as stated*

Standing here on the edge
Of something big,
Something unsettling,
Walking on eggshells--
        Crack*ling*, *...ling,...ling,...ling*,
        Crunch*ing*, *ing, ing, ing*
        Crumbl*ing*, *bling,bling,bling*

Along the path,
        *Crackle,....crackle,*
        *...crunch,*
        *...crunch*
        *...crumble*
        *...crumble*

*B e y o n d* days
Displayed as a *"Dali"-esque* melting of time and space,
Bending, morphing, amorphous
Without stomach or soul involved

## At the Concert

*Metaphorically...*
This creamy, day-dreamy night
Tucked into the middle of July,
Electric, the mood of families
As they connect with one another,
*...Merging generations,*
*...Merging voices*
A Beatles' tune plays
On the steps of Crane's Mansion
At Castle Hill

Sweeping vistas of sparkling sea and sand,
Massive, manicured meadows
Undulating, rolling green
And sweeping toward the sea

Thousands of people
Sporting brilliant colors
Dot the expansive lawn
As it spills its way toward the sea
Indiscernible specks of humanity
On blankets and chaise lounges
Wine the aphrodisiac

Beatles bellow ballads of long ago and far away
Piercing the air
Proclaiming a "Revolution"
Memories of the 60's
Of long ago – *of "Yesterday"*
But clearly alive--
*If only for today.*

# Of Conventions ... and Cotton Candy

Numbing, antiseptic,
Convention *drills*–
Cotton candy, sticky sweet,
Bracing, dangerous, intolerant

No mediation of ideas
Ideas packaged for easy digestion
An impossible disconnect
Fragmented and distanced from the reality
of the middle class

Beautiful people, lusciously summoned
To tell tales of a perfect family
A perfect marriage
Instead of the dense complexities of American life

Conventions bristle with the magic of media mongering
Tweeting trivialities
Instead of authentic American issues
People, torn asunder by joblessness, instant poverty,
intolerance

Hopelessly torn political parties
Clouded by moral contradiction
Categorically dismissive
In denial of what it means
For policy to follow authentic needs
Of real people, caught in the middle

Cotton candy, see through politics--
Exterior, pink, promising
Internally, a pile of dissolving nothingness,
Cotton candy disguised as substance

Where marionette style delegates are pulled and prodded
By the elite one percent
Clouding and confusing **the** American people
Obliterating the American dream

## Waiting to Serve

*Soothing, soothing,*
Floating on air and *soothing*
The grey fog of summer
Grey, *soothing*, beckoning-
*This* room, soaking up the sea
In a *soothing* grey bath

*Beckoning* visitors through French doors
Opened wide
Not half way, but fully opened--
And *beckoning*, gently calling
*Beckoning* friends and family, or a family of friends
Friendly on a foggy, grey day at the sea

Round table ready, waiting *patiently*
Set for four
Friends, or family, or family not friends
Or friends not family, or both!

Gently *beckoning*, fog and candlelight
Merging, where merging is mixing readily
And readily mixing

Candles *ready*, but yet to be lit
Neither grand chandelier nor candles glowing
But *ready*--

As *ready* is often just *waiting* and *beckoning* gently
With no pretense,
Silently, with no rush—but *ready*,
Now!

Time, time for friends and family
Or friends or family
To join together
Connecting
Sitting, not standing
But visiting and dining in deck chairs
Not formal and stuffed with cotton
But casual not stuffy
As friends and family or friends or family are not stuffy
But invited into this beautiful place
To dine by the sea

Not seeing what is not there
As fog enshrouds
But what could be there
And which might or might not be there
Depending upon the clarity of lenses
From which families as friends
See the beauty of this place and this life
Through the soft and hazy lenses of family and friends
Or friends or family or family friends
Beckoning --*from this dining room by the sea*
*Patiently waiting*
*And ready to "serve".*

# *...Sist...Sist...Sister, Pick Me!*

"Sist...Sist...Sist..." That's the call of the devoted Catholic school student, begging to answer a question to impress Sister! It was like a chorus of banshees trying to show off their knowledge, gleaned through sweaty brows of the previous night's study session! It really didn't matter what the answer was, but was more about the sounds that were made. And it seemed Sister was oblivious to their and my pleading, almost agonizing calls for attention. After all, how DO you fairly call on about 61 eager students competing by waving arms and hands while stretching impossibly from their seats to reach Sister, perched on the edge of her desk. The desk was displayed squarely on a two foot high wooden platform in the front of the class.

In any public school, this chaotic enthusiasm would have been rewarded by a teacher's delirious joy at the prospect of students eager to share what had been learned the night before. But not here though! Catholic school children gone mad! Boys and girls alike, stretching their seated bodies into twisted pretzels as if to greet some rock star, instead of the menacing presence in the front who rewarded such enthusiasm with a stoic look of distain, as if to say, "You had better know that answer!"

We had all come to the conclusion that we were probably chanting "Sist...Sist...Sist..." and waving wildly because it had come to symbolize a ritualistic show of, "I've studied, and I want you to acknowledge me!" Those who "Sist-ed" the longest and loudest, it was assumed had studied the hardest -into the wee hours of the morning.

I was among them. Since we were chastised for screaming, I perfected my cries into a wailing and blistering "Sist" almost a death cry! Effective, I thought, but to no avail.

With 61 wailing kids, both boys and girls in our eight grade class, it was a highly inefficient way for Sister to conduct a lesson.

"Sist... Sist...," I exclaimed, a hard snake-like hiss enunciating the call. "Please pick me! I'm prepared."

So, Sister instituted a set of name calling cards. This large stack of white paper-stock quality cards, sat neatly tied with one elastic band (a rubber band to non-New Englanders) straining to keep 61 name calling cards in an upright position. And there you have it. ... Tidy, efficient, white, business-like cards, shuffled regularly at the beginning of class each day. In fact, it was the first thing Sister did after class began.

We were all used to the whirling sounds the shuffled cards made in the hands of a highly skilled shuffler. Perfectly executed. Sister could have played a mean game of Poker if she played cards, which we all supposed she did NOT. But looking back on eight grade from where I sit today, she did have a Poker face that no one in the class would have disputed!

You would think this to be the end of the story, but it's only just the beginning. You see, Sister never counted the number of cards in the pile nor did she ever notice the pile dwindling throughout that month of October. But I can assure you I felt gipped that year. I was too timid to play the game! ...until the opportunity literally fell into my lap.

Here's how it all happened: One day in early October, Sister's elastic band, old and fragile from years of wear, broke!!! Sister just left the name cards stacked high and straight at the edge of her desk as always. Then it happened! Just as the lunch bell sounded, Joey walked by Sister's desk and "accidentally" knocked over the complete stack of name cards with his elbow. They scattered everywhere like confetti. Joey made a beeline to straighten up the cards, making sure each name was faced correctly. The rest of us, and Sister, were anxiously waiting for our dismissal to lunch. We ALL saw it, all but Sister that is. Between the height of the platform and the desk obstructing her view, only the students were privy to what happened next. Joey, slyly and without missing a beat, slipped his own name card up his sleeve! He placed the cards in a nice neat pile on Sister's desk and lined up like the rest of us. That might have been the first time I saw Sister crack a smile. Joey was a quiet boy, long and awkward, a typical boy of 13 years old.

But Joey wasn't the brightest bulb on the tree and between his shyness and not studying as much as he needed to, Joey felt he would be safe from the "name calling" by Sister. Little did Joey realize just how many of us actually saw his feat of "magic". Make the name card go away, and never have to study for the rest of the year! Now, Sister would surely notice a card missing from the pile!

Well, October passed uneventfully, and Sister never did call Joey's name. And she never even noticed that Joey wasn't called on. Well, Joey even got up the nerve to stammer, "Sist...Sist...Sister." And by the end of October, he knew he was home free. It looked like he studied, for he pleaded to be called by Sister, but as "luck" (NOT!!!) would have it, Joey just smiled and relaxed in class.

Throughout the month of October, Sister failed to secure the name calling cards with a new elastic band. Those students who had witnessed Joey make his name card magically disappear, one-by-one, skillfully extorted their names from the pile, ensuring a comfortable stint in Sister's class for the entire eight grade year.

The girls in the class, bound by honor but mostly by fear of getting caught, didn't try removing their names.

All but me that is, and only by accident—or the grace or disgrace of God!  Shy, sweet, study-until-you-drop me!  It happened so naturally.  Sister approached me one day after the students were dismissed for lunch and handed me a wider, new elastic band with instructions to straighten up the name cards and then rubber band them.

"What?" ...Opportunity knocked, and I was aghast!

"Thanks, Sister," I mumbled, and set to work.  There was my name, typed and right there in my hand.  I had fantasized about a moment like this. What a fantastic opportunity... to take my name out of the pile!  A wave of relief washed over me at the thought of no more pressure to answer to Sister for the rest of the year!

I even counted the name cards.  I noticed the dwindling pile.  ...Ten short of the 61.  Surely Sister should have noticed by now!  Trembling, I took my name card out of the pile and slipped it into my jacket pocket.  I then placed the elastic band snuggly around the name cards, and proceeded to lunch.

Instead of the rush of victory coursing through my veins, the name card weighed me down like a ten ton boulder in my pocket. My pocket was now a burden and my conscience screamed out-"Cheater"!

Should I confess? Tell Sister what I knew about the other 10 cheaters too?

Upon returning to class, Sister got right to work, and I was safe from her scrutiny. I felt relieved. Only I still wasn't happy. I still studied each night, but now I wasn't playing by the rules. I felt miserable.

I never did have an opportunity to replace the name card back, which was my intended plan to ease my own guilty conscience. But I studied hard and in class I still called out wildly: "Sist...Sist...Sister", and each time, I looked over at Joey who had started the whole thing. By May, he was an Oscar contender, but I decided to play it a bit more prudently.

And I suspect that those ten students who "Sist-ed" the loudest were the very ones who were the safest from the name card caller—Sister!

*Confessional Poem:*
*May God Strike You Dead!*

*I.*

Looking back on this harrowing third grade experience,
I smile as I tell this story. But I assure you, *it was no
laughing matter at the time!*

I was a helper-shy- but always trying to please Sister.
In third grade, I could tell, Sister and I hit it off! I didn't
live far from St. Mary's Grammar School, just up over
the hill and down a long city block, so Mom frequently
allowed me to stay after school to help straighten out
our third grade classroom.  After all, there were chalk
boards to be erased and washed, and erasers to be
clapped, outside of course.

I recall that day long ago because of the consequences
to my psyche that have lasted a lifetime! Sister
requested that I "tidy" (as she called it) all the desks
so that papers were not hanging from the desks.  She
always liked a neat classroom. I was thrilled to take
on a brand new task!  Up and down the aisles I flew,
straightening and tidying like a seven year old pro!

I remember finding a nickel in one of the messy desks.
I remember it clearly. I turned that nickel over and over
in my hand, fingered the buffalo's raised image and

contemplated just what I could buy with that magical nickel. I had never stolen anything in all my seven years.

*...Just this once?  ...Who would miss it, right?*

I gave myself permission to steal, as I rationalized the theft.  I settled on a candy bar and slipped the nickel in my shoe. We didn't have pockets in our blue uniforms. I kept my eye laser fixed on Sister's every move as I deftly and with an elephant sitting on my chest, stole that nickel on that fateful afternoon. This one act set into motion a series of consequences that would be forever seared into my memory.

Immediate gratification sure should feel great.  That candy bar was in my stomach, devoured, within five minutes of clearing the building.

*What's a kid to do, right?*
*Who would miss a nickel right?*
*I would take this ugly act of stealing to the grave with me,* I vowed!

WRONG!  DEAD WRONG!!!

*II.*

I had set the wheels into motion. The next day, the guilt of stealing the nickel weighed me down.  I, we the class, I mean, were greeted by a somber, imposing third grade teacher. Arms crossed, garb black as the night, and the crucifix of Jesus affixed to the rosary beads Sister wore around her waist was staring at me, eye level. I knew something was up, and I, unlike the rest of my class, knew exactly what that something was!

*Hands folded*, bellowed Sister, and we prayed first. I said that prayer as though my little life depended on it—and it did as I later would come to realize!

Sister laid out the scenario: Someone among us was a "thief", and she wanted to know who that someone was!

All morning, we were grilled. I didn't break! I was terrified; remember how shy I told you I was? I was in deeper with every action Sister used to ferret out the thief.

> *Did we know that stealing was a sin?*
> *...a venial sin?...or was it a mortal sin?* I wondered?
> *Would I go to hell for stealing this nickel?*
> *I promise, if I am not caught, God, I will NEVER, EVER Steal anything again.*

The words and the promise to God were deliberate and heartfelt. Surely *HE* would hear my prayer!

*Did we know that this nickel belonged to David, and that he now didn't have enough money to buy his lunch today?*

*I didn't know that!*

*Could it get any worse?* It did!

No recess! That was the least of my worries! I would miss recess *all* year, if Sister would stop her relentless pursuit to ferret me out! I was knee deep now!

We each received a blank piece of paper. All the person who stole the nickel needed to do was to write his/her—my—name on the blank paper and Sister would forgive and not punish that person. *Right!* Sounded too easy to me! I wasn't buying it!

Now that everyone knew there was a thief among us who had stolen food money from David, I would never survive a confession. I slipped the blank paper into the bucket along with everyone else and waited. Sister, slowly and deliberately, *and* dramatically—I might add—opened each piece of paper and by the last blank piece of paper, I could tell she was furious.

I wasn't about to crack now! Not in front of God, Sister, my friends– and David!

*Sorry, David, if I would have known this was your lunch money, I would have left it alone!*

The lunch bell screamed out; it temporarily stopped the torture. ***Maybe I was safe! NO SUCH LUCK!!...WITH CAPITALS!!!!***

Why didn't Sister just give up! She was a bulldog and getting more tenacious by the hour. End of the day! I thought it was over, finally! Little did I know Sister had done last trick up her proverbial sleeve!

*And this one would make me crack!* I was fragile and sweaty by now.

*Get on with it, Sister!*

It had now begun to rain, not just ordinary, light, gentle rain, but *Wrath of God* rain, and I thought I heard the groan of thunder too!

Only ten more minutes and school would be over. How bad could it get? *REALLY BAD!!!*

***III.***

Sister's plan was simple:
Each row (and there were eight rows) would stand. One by one we would approach the holy water font (a plastic font of water with a molded face of Jesus staring back at us) in the front of the classroom, screwed into the doorframe. We would dip a single finger into the holy water, and then make the sign of the cross.

*That sounded easy*, I thought.

Well, here's the catch–
Sister proclaimed that the person who had stolen the nickel, if they took the holy water, and if they made the sign of the cross, God would strike him or her– ME– DEAD!!  Yes,  that's right, dead on the spot, right there at the holy water font!

I froze…and counted the rows.
Row 1 stood.  I was in Row 6 of 8 rows.  One by one the torture began.  Silence within, thunder and ferocious rain outside the classroom window.
Row 2, 3, 4, 5…

Now, Row 6, and I, last in the row!  We stand! My heart pounded so hard I was unable to concentrate on anything else.  My palms were sweaty, and I felt lightheaded! I trembled and sobbed silent tears of repentance.

*…My turn.  I could do this!*

**JUST** as I was about to reach for the holy water, the largest crack of lightning God ever created struck somewhere close by, and you guessed it!

I literally fell to the ground shrieking:  *"I did it; I stole the nickel!"*

I was inconsolable. I bet my tears equaled the dearth of rain falling outside. I knew stealing was a bad idea, but I'm only seven, and God is going to condemn me to the fires of hell—*right now! This minute!!!*

Sister, knowing now what role she had played in her sinister plot, ran to my side just as the end of the day bell rang. I couldn't stop wailing...*not* for an hour... *not* even when they called Mother Superior and she called my Mother to come to school to get me ...*not* all that night ...*not* even in my Mother's consoling arms.

...And to this day? You guessed it: I've never stolen anything.. ***and I don't like nickels!...never have, never will!***
...and that's the truth, really!

# Of Course I Ate the Chocolate!

When you placed that piece of luscious chocolate pie, topped with whipped cream, down beside me, what did you think would happen?

### I.

### ...of course I ate the chocolate!

As a child I ate a box of x-lax, stashed high upon a refrigerator, safe from most children, but not from me. At seven, I could climb like a monkey, and dark chocolate spoke to me, so I ate it, not thinking about the consequences, not realizing that vomiting and a trip to the emergency room would be in my immediate future.

### II.

### ...of course I ate the chocolate!

Even as an adult, I craved the taste, salivated over the prospects of picking out small, irregular chunks from the vanilla ice cream. I'd leave the vanilla smashed along the sides of the cardboard container, my mission, the blotchy, miniscule pieces pitched on the container itself, as chocolate chunks. The picture alone gave me pause for salivating . I could picture diving into the ice cream, using my thumb and index fingers to pick out the flecks of chocolate, and feeling the flavorful properties of that dark chocolate, lingering in my mouth until the entire experience was complete, but not until I carefully licked my fingers, and emitted the ultimate squeaks and "mmm's" for a proper appreciation, and for maximizing this sensuous buzz of contentment.

### III.

### *...of course I ate the chocolate!*

Why wouldn't I? I had a "GET OUT OF JAIL FREE" card. After all, I *WAS* pregnant. And I was pregnant three times, or a whopping 27 months. Chocolate clung to my pony tail and stained my maternity clothes. I inhaled chocolate everywhere...

My particular favorite was chocolate donuts, with chocolate coating, and topped with chocolate sprinkles! ... and I always bought two of them, donuts of course. I freely dove into those chocolate donuts, especially at nine months pregnant when people knew to not "upset the pregnant lady". Dark pieces of sugary brown splotches landed randomly on my bloated belly.

What a sight as I painstakingly extracted every crumb from the creases of my large, very large, man shirt. I sat in my favorite rocker, swollen feet raised high, and feeling every bit entitled to each morsel. I savored the taste... I developed a ritual for eating chocolate donuts which continued every single day for the entire ninth month of my pregnancy. First, I would bit off a small portion of chocolate donut using my front teeth. Then I would place the bite ritualistically on the roof of my mouth and swirl it with my tongue, rubbing it against my inner cheeks, enjoying the lingering flavor and engaging all my senses. I would smell the aroma wafting from the inside of my mouth, run my tongue across its smoothness as I, by now, had pulverized it into mush. My time to relax; my time to feed my unborn baby. Since the Dunkin Donut store was just down the hill from my house, I would walk down during the day, about 6:00pm, and buy my two chocolate donuts for the next day. Naturally, I hid them, behind my winter wardrobe where no man would go, and where they would be safe until the next morning!

## IV.

### ...of course I ate the chocolate!

Especially during the Valentine season, which, for me, started on February 1, and continued long after the holiday! No one need ask what to get me! But I was flexible. I must admit though, I have a special preference for dark chocolate and nuts. What a combination! What a perfect excuse for a chocolate binge! Using the pointer finger of my right hand-the only finger with a strong nail—I would depress the nail into the bottom of each careful arrangement of

Belgian chocolate to double check the richness and darkness of each little chocolate nugget as it rested in that lovely heart shaped box. Of course I thought I was being cagey! I thought by hiding the marked pieces of chocolate no one would be able to tell just how desperate I was to dive into the chocolates. But as it always turned out, I ended up eating my favorites first, my second favorites next, and by the time I finished playing my little game of "just one more piece", I was desperately eating the ugly chocolates that I vowed I would not eat-ever! I must confess to mutilating the lovely candy box now and then when it did not open quickly enough for my palate's sake. If calories could be reversed every time I ate chocolate, I would be pencil thin. I am not*! ...of course I ate the chocolate!... all of it! I wallowed in the flavor and swallowed it in one gulp!*

# Lilacs and the Scent of My Mother

I stretch my body between the sheets, almost feeling the earth beneath me. I dig my heels deep into the fabric and burrow, waiting for this feeling of peace and comfort to consume me. Nestling into the bed like a newborn nesting into its mother's breast, I am cozy under down comforter and peaceful colors of eggplant and lilac. *Always lilac.*

I can almost smell the purple lilac walls as they hug me in this tiny bedroom, too small for most people, but not for me. Soothing purple, coursing through my veins, helping me remember my mother. Lilac was her favorite color, maybe because of her favorite perfume, *Lilies of the Valley.* It had a fruity scent, but my mother always thought of lilacs when she wore that perfume. Maybe a contradiction of flowers, but definitely her.

I remember the heart shaped container that my mother gave me, long after the perfume bottles were empty. It was elegant, sturdy, and achingly beautiful to this ten year old birthday girl. The cardboard box was dazzling, almost magical, a marketing feat in the late fifties, designed for the woman who wanted more than just perfume, designed for the woman who wanted to feel loved and beautiful, even before the box was opened.

The scent was my mother, *The Lilies of the Valley*

perfume scent she loved, and housed in the gift box I remember her using for as long as I *could* remember. Passing that gift on to me as part of my turning that big number, ten, made me feel like a princess. Long after she realized she could not afford to buy this perfume any longer, she still devoured the scent and used the box for her costume jewelry. I always remember her delight as she opened the box and lingered first, basking in the aroma of this lovely fruity scent. It was the same ritual every morning as I peeked around the corner, capturing that moment, etched forever in my mind. After years of wear, the box still looked pristine. The inside, lined with a lilac silk, was carefully preserved with the softest touch of her hands, knowing it would be passed on to me when the time was ready.

The time was ready the day I turned ten. My mother had built up the significance of this birthday well in advance. Nestled under the covers with mother's arm around me, I knew my life would forever change.

The smell was instant spring in a box. I remember immediately transferring of all my treasured possessions into that box on my tenth birthday. Into the box went my Cinderella watch, the pocket necklace my mother had given me earlier in the day, her picture on one side, facing mine on the other side. Also, in that box I transferred my baseball cars, banded by a red rubber band, with the Mickey Mantle card on top.

It was a hybrid assortment of precious "stuff" collected and sorted with the utmost of care. But every time I opened that heart shaped box, I took a deep penetrating breath of *Lilies of the Valley*. That scent must have seeped into the fibers of that box long ago and is forever seared into my soul. Just the mere anticipation of that scent became the reason to open the box.

I am not surprised that I feel comfortable with a Lilac room. I smile back, feeling protected, and drift off to sleep, hugged by my lilac walls and the unseen presence of my mother.

Made in the USA
Charleston, SC
06 November 2014